Elizabeth Tayntor Gowell

Whales and Dolphins

What They Have in Common

Franklin Watts - A Division of Grolier Publishing
New York • London • Hong Kong • Sydney • Danbury, Connecticut

For Jay

Visit Franklin Watts on the Internet at:
http://publishing.grolier.com

Library of Congress Cataloging-in-Publication Data

Gowell, Elizabeth Tayntor.
Whales and dolphins: what they have in common / Elizabeth Tayntor Gowell.
    p. cm. — (Animals in order)
    Includes bibliographical references and index.
    Summary: Describes the traits and classification of the aquatic mammals called cetaceans, with an emphasis on different kinds of dolphins and whales.
    ISBN 0-531-20396-4 (lib. bdg.)   0-531-16454-3 (pbk.)
    1. Whales—Juvenile literature. 2. Dolphins— Juvenile literature. [1. Whales. 2. Dolphins. 3. Cetaceans.] I. Title. II. Series.
QL737.C4G59   1999
599.5—dc21   98-25754
                                                    CIP

Contents

What Is a Cetacean?

Have you ever seen a dolphin in a movie or a television show? Maybe you've seen a live one at a zoo or an aquarium.

You probably know that dolphins live in the ocean. They never come out of the water. However, dolphins are unlike many other animals that live in the ocean. Dolphins belong to a special group, or *order*, of animals called *cetaceans*.

Dolphins are not the only cetaceans in the world. Whales and porpoises also belong to the order.

Two of the animals shown on the opposite page are cetaceans, and two are not. Can you guess which are not cetaceans?

Blue shark

Spotted dolphin

Orca

Florida manatee

Traits of a Cetacean

Did you choose the shark and the manatee? You were right! How can you tell they are not cetaceans?

Cetaceans live in water, but they are not fish. They are *mammals.* Cetaceans have lungs and must swim to the surface of the water to breathe air. They are warm-blooded and feed their babies with mother's milk, just as humans do. Unlike most mammals, cetaceans don't have fur or hair. Cetaceans have smooth skin. A layer of fat, or *blubber,* underneath the skin keeps them warm.

A cetacean's long, pointed body glides easily through the water. Instead of arms and legs, a cetacean has *flippers* and a tail with powerful fins called *flukes.* The flukes move up and down, not side to side. That design gives cetaceans the power to dive deeply and then return to the surface quickly to breathe.

Like other cetaceans, this humpback whale has flippers and a fluke.

A family of orcas

A female cetacean usually has only one baby at a time. A baby cetacean can swim right after birth. Sometimes the mother has to help her baby to the surface for its first breath. Cetacean mothers stay with their babies for about 1 year. The mothers feed and protect the babies until they are big enough to take care of themselves.

Most cetaceans are *carnivores*—they eat other animals. A few eat *plankton*, a sort of ocean "soup" made up of tiny floating animals and plants.

Cetaceans live in all the oceans of the world. Some even spend time in freshwater rivers. Some cetaceans live in warm water; others live in cold water. When the seasons change, many cetaceans travel hundreds or even thousands of miles to find the food and water temperatures they need to survive.

The Order of Living Things

A tiger has more in common with a house cat than with a daisy. A true bug is more like a butterfly than a jellyfish. Scientists arrange living things into groups based on how they look and how they act. A tiger and a house cat belong to the same group, but a daisy belongs to a different group.

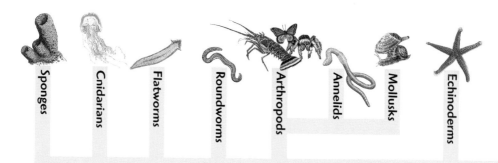

Sponges • Cnidarians • Flatworms • Roundworms • Arthropods • Annelids • Mollusks • Echinoderms

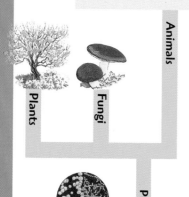

Animals • Plants • Fungi • Protists • Monerans

All living things can be placed in one of five groups called *kingdoms*: the plant kingdom, the animal kingdom, the fungus kingdom, the moneran kingdom, or the protist kingdom. You can probably name many of the creatures in the plant and animal kingdoms. The fungus kingdom includes mushrooms, yeasts, and molds. The moneran and protist kingdoms contain thousands of living things that are too small to see without a microscope.

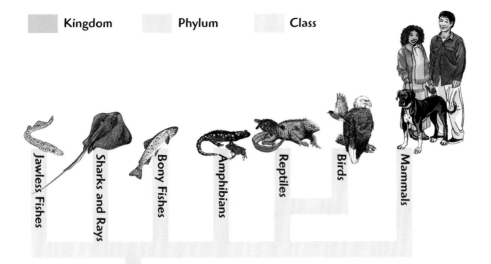

Kingdom | Phylum | Class

Jawless Fishes
Sharks and Rays
Bony Fishes
Amphibians
Reptiles
Birds
Mammals

Chordates

Because there are millions and millions of living things on Earth, some of the members of one kingdom may not seem all that similar. The animal kingdom includes creatures as different as tarantulas and trout, jellyfish and jaguars, salamanders and sparrows, elephants and earthworms.

To show that an elephant is more like a jaguar than an earthworm, scientists further separate the creatures in each kingdom into more specific groups. The animal kingdom can be divided into nine *phyla*. Humans belong to the chordate phylum. Almost all chordates have a backbone.

Each phylum can be subdivided into many *classes*. Humans, mice, and elephants all belong to the *mammal* class. Each class can be further divided into orders; orders into *families*, families into *genera*, and genera into *species*. All the members of a species are very similar.

How Cetaceans Fit In

You can probably guess that cetaceans belong to the animal kingdom. They have much more in common with bears and bats than with maple trees and morning glories.

Cetaceans belong to the chordate phylum. Almost all chordates have a backbone and a skeleton. Can you think of other chordates? Examples include elephants, mice, snakes, birds, fish, and humans.

The chordate phylum has a number of classes. Cetaceans belong to the mammal class. Elephants, humans, dogs, and cats are all mammals.

There are seventeen orders of mammals. Cetaceans are one of those orders. The name "cetacean" comes from the Greek word *ketos*, which means "whale."

Cetaceans are divided into two suborders, the odontocetes and the mysticetes. Odontocetes are cetaceans with teeth. They include dolphins, porpoises, and toothed whales. Mysticetes do not have teeth. Instead, they use comblike strainers called *baleen* to capture their food. Baleen is made of the same material as human fingernails. The name "mysticete" means "mustached whale."

Cetaceans can be further divided into a number of families and genera. There are about ninety species of cetaceans. You will learn about some of those species in this book.

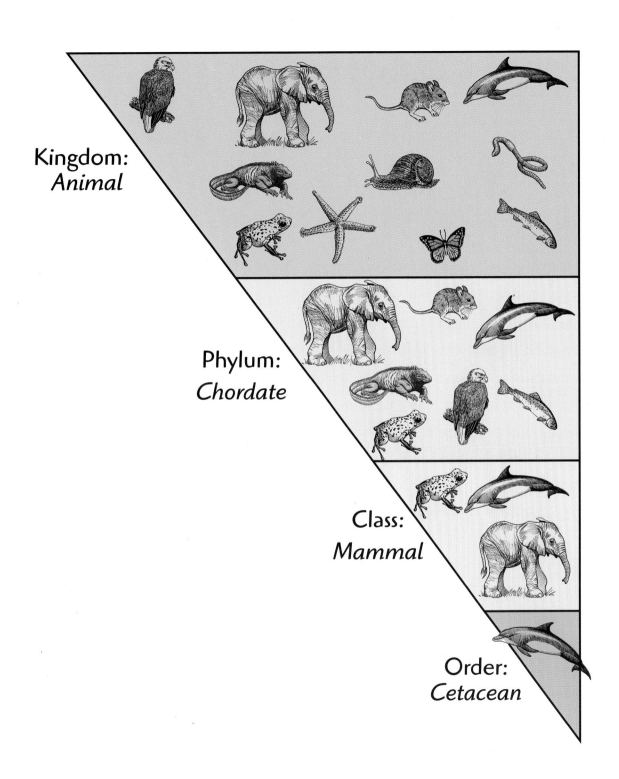

Kingdom:
Animal

Phylum:
Chordate

Class:
Mammal

Order:
Cetacean

Bottlenose Dolphins

FAMILY: Delphinidae
COMMON NAME: Bottlenose dolphin
GENUS AND SPECIES: *Tursiops truncatus*
SIZE: Up to 12 feet (3.5 m) long; 440 pounds (200 kg)

Have you ever seen dolphins performing at an aquarium? They might have been bottlenose dolphins, one of the most familiar of all cetaceans.

A bottlenose dolphin breathes through a *blowhole* on the top of its head. The dolphin opens its blowhole to take in air. Then the blowhole closes automatically to keep the water out. It's like a built-in nose plug. Bottlenose dolphins can hold their breath for 15 minutes.

When bottlenose dolphins hunt for fish and squid, they use a special sense called *echolocation*. As a dolphin swims, it sends out clicking sounds. When those sounds hit a fish or another object, they bounce back to the dolphin. The dolphin uses the echoes to find the object. If you threw a dime into a deep pool, a dolphin could find and retrieve it before it hit the bottom—even blindfolded!

Bottlenose dolphins live together in family groups of ten to twenty-five animals. Members of a group help one another. They may help an injured dolphin to the surface so it can breathe or protect it from enemies. When a baby dolphin is born, other dolphins sometimes help the mother get her baby to the surface for its first breath. Bottlenose dolphins live for up to 30 years.

Spotted Dolphins

FAMILY: Delphinidae
COMMON NAME: Spotted dolphin
GENUS AND SPECIES: *Stenella attenuata*
SIZE: Up to 7 feet (2 m) long; 220 pounds (100 kg)

Spotted dolphins live in warm waters all over the world. They are born gray, but as they grow up, spots appear on their backs and bellies. Spotted dolphins are the fastest of all the dolphins. They can swim as fast as 25 miles (40 km) per hour.

Spotted dolphins sometimes form schools made up of thousands of leaping, splashing animals. Large schools of yellowfin tuna sometimes follow the dolphins. People who fish for tuna use the dolphins to help them find fish. When these fishers see a large school of spotted dolphins, they know tuna are nearby. The fishers drop their nets in a circle surrounding the dolphins and pull up their catch. They catch lots of tuna using this technique. Unfortunately, they also catch spotted dolphins. The fishers free the dolphins as soon as they can, but many dolphins drown in the nets.

Some tuna companies do not buy yellowfin tuna. Others buy yellowfin tuna only from fishers who use special nets that let the dolphins escape. When you buy cans of tuna, look for a label that says the tuna is "dolphin safe." That means dolphins were not harmed when the tuna was caught.

15

River Dolphins

FAMILY: Platanistidae
COMMON EXAMPLE: Amazon River dolphin
GENUS AND SPECIES: *Inia geoffrensis*
SIZE: Up to 10 feet (3 m) long; 340 pounds (154 kg)

Deep in the Amazon River basin of South America, the water is the color of chocolate. In the surrounding rain forest, toucans and parrots screech, and insects buzz. A dugout canoe glides through the dark water. Below the water's surface swim animals so secretive that scientists once thought they were only legends. Then, snorting and puffing, they surface. They are Amazon River dolphins.

Each year when the Amazon River floods, water covers the forest floor. This makes it possible for dolphins to swim among the trees where jaguars normally prowl. Sometimes the dolphins gather in groups to hunt fish. At other times, they travel alone or in small family groups of two or three.

The Amazon River dolphin has very small eyes and a long tube-shaped snout

lined with teeth. Scientists think the animals use echolocation to hunt in the murky river waters. An adult Amazon River dolphin eats up to 10 pounds (4.5 kg) of fish per day.

Species of river dolphins also live in China and India. Although river dolphins are protected all over the world, they sometimes drown in fishing nets or die when boats hit them. The biggest threat to their survival is pollution and loss of their wild river habitat.

Porpoises

FAMILY: Phocoenidae
COMMON EXAMPLE: Harbor porpoise
GENUS AND SPECIES: *Phocoena phocoena*
SIZE: Up to 6 feet (2 m) long; 120 pounds (54 kg)

Snorting and puffing, a group of harbor porpoises swims along the coast. Some people call these small cetaceans sea pigs because they make so much noise. Harbor porpoises live in the cool coastal waters of the Atlantic and Pacific oceans. They are fast swimmers but not deep divers. They can hold their breath for about 4 minutes.

Newborn harbor porpoise calves are half the size of their mothers. The calves drink mother's milk for about 12 months. During that time, mother porpoises protect their young from sharks and killer whales.

Other species of porpoises also take good care of their young. The Chinese finless porpoise carries her baby on her back. A patch of rough skin provides a nonskid place for the calf to ride.

How can you tell the difference between a porpoise and a dolphin? Scientists look at the teeth. Dolphins have sharp, cone-shaped teeth. Porpoises have blunt teeth shaped like a spade or a chisel. There are only a few species of true porpoises. All other toothed cetaceans are either dolphins or small whales.

19

Sperm Whales

FAMILY: Physeteridae

COMMON NAME: Sperm whale

GENUS AND SPECIES: *Physeter catodon*

SIZE: Males up to 62 feet (19 m) long; 40,000 pounds (18,000 kg);

Females up to 39 feet (12 m) long; 13,300 pounds (6,000 kg)

A sperm whale takes several breaths, then dives—down, down, down toward the depths. About 5,000 feet (1,500 m) beneath the surface, the huge mammal senses prey. A giant squid hovers just ahead. The whale's eyes are as big as basketballs, but it can't see the squid in the darkness. Echolocation tells the whale where to find the prey. With a powerful stroke of its flukes, the whale lunges forward and grabs the squid in its jaws.

Sperm whales are the largest of the toothed whales. A full-grown male can eat 1,000 pounds (450 kg) of squid each day. Most of its food is bite-sized, but sometimes sperm whales go after big prey. A 10-foot (3-m) shark was once found in a sperm whale's stomach!

Sperm whales dive deeper than any other cetaceans. They can hold their breath for 2 hours and dive to a depth of almost 2 miles (3 km).

A sperm whale's huge head makes up 25 to 35 percent of its total body length. A special oil called spermaceti fills the head. In the past, the oil was very valuable because it was used to power lamps.

Whalers also valued the sperm whale's teeth. Sailors carved intricate designs called scrimshaw onto the teeth. Today the sperm whale is protected by international law. It is illegal to hunt them anywhere in the world.

Orcas

FAMILY: Delphinidae
COMMON NAME: Orca
GENUS AND SPECIES: *Orcinus orca*
SIZE: Males up to 30 feet (9 m) long; 12,000 pounds (5,400 kg);
  Females up to 23 feet (7 m) long; 8,000 pounds (3,600 kg)

The surface water whirls amd boils as black fins slice through the sea. Twenty hungry orcas attack a school of fish. These black-and-white whales live in all the oceans of the world. They often travel together in groups called *pods*. Orcas swim up to 30 miles (48 km) per hour. They can leap 20 feet (6 m) into the air.

Orcas are fierce hunters. Their sharp teeth help them catch squid, seals,penguins, sea turtles, and other marine animals. Orcas even attack and kill other large whales. Because they sometimes attack and kill when they are not hungry, orcas are also called killer whales.

Although orcas are dangerous to other ocean animals, no one has ever reported an orca attack on a human. If you have ever seen orcas in an aquarium or in the movies, you may think of them as gentle animals. Animal trainers have taught some orcas to let a person reach inside their mouths to touch their teeth and tongue.

Baby orcas are black and white, just like their parents. Newborn calves are 9 feet (2.5 m) long and weigh 400 pounds (180 kg). The baby whales stay with their mothers and feed on mother's milk for about 1 year. Orcas can live to be more than 35 years old.

Narwhals

FAMILY: Monodontidae

COMMON NAME: Narwhal

GENUS AND SPECIES: *Monodon monoceros*

SIZE: Up to 15 feet (4.5 m) long; 3,000 pounds (1,350 kg)

Do you believe in unicorns? Unicorn horses exist only in fairy tales, but real, live unicorns swim in the sea. These animals are called narwhals, or unicorn whales.

Narwhals have only two teeth. When a male narwhal is about a year old, one of the teeth, usually the one on the left, begins to grow. Eventually, it grows through the narwhal's upper lip. The tooth keeps growing until it forms a long spiral tusk. In an adult male, the tusk can be 8 feet (2.5 m) long.

Scientists think that male narwhals use their tusks to attract females. The biggest and strongest males usually have the longest tusks. During mating season, the males hit their tusks against one another, like knights in a sword fight. Some narwhals break their tusks in those battles.

Narwhals eat squid, fish, crabs, and shrimp. The whales are bluish gray or light brown with leopardlike spots. Narwhals live only in the Arctic Ocean. Sometimes they swim close to shore in bays and shallow waters.

Usually only male narwhals grow tusks, although researchers have reported a few females with tusks. Very rarely, a male or a female may have two large tusks.

Pilot Whales

FAMILY: Delphinidae

COMMON EXAMPLE: Long-finned pilot whale

GENUS AND SPECIES: *Globicephala melaena*

SIZE: Males up to 26 feet (8 m) long; 7,000 pounds (3,200 kg);

Females up to 20 feet (6 m) long; 6,000 pounds (2,700 kg)

Pilot whales are black, with bellies that range from cream to gray. These medium-sized whales usually live in coastal waters and often move into bays and harbors to feed. Pilot whales usually travel in groups. Sometimes they follow a leader, or pilot. They are named for that trait.

Following the leader may also be why pilot whales sometimes swim into shallow water and strand themselves on the beach at low tide. Sometimes just one pilot whale gets stuck. At other times, dozens of whales are stranded.

Like all cetaceans, pilot whales die if they are out of the water for a long time. People often try to save beached pilot whales by lifting them off the beach and guiding them into deeper water. Some of the rescued animals swim away. But, for unknown reasons, others follow the leader back up onto the beach and strand themselves again.

Scientists don't know why pilot whales will follow a leader to their death. Maybe they are trying to help a sick comrade. Maybe their echolocation stops working along shallow coastlines. Parasites, ear infections, or other illnesses may also be involved.

Pilot whales are not the only cetaceans that beach themselves. Dolphins, porpoises, and other whales also show this strange behavior.

Belugas

FAMILY: Monodontidae
COMMON NAME: Beluga
GENUS AND SPECIES: *Delphinapterus leucas*
SIZE: Up to 18 feet (5.5 m) long; 1,100 pounds (500 kg)

At the edge of the Arctic Ocean, a white head pops up through a hole in the ice. It's a beluga, the white whale of the north. The name "beluga" comes from the Russian word *belukha*, which means "white." The whale's lack of color helps it hide from enemies in the icy white regions of the world. The beluga takes a few quick breaths, then disappears again beneath the ice.

Belugas visit breathing holes wherever the sea freezes. Without breathing holes, the whales would drown underneath the ice. But breathing holes also mean danger. Hungry polar bears often wait beside the holes. When a beluga comes up for air, the bears attack. Scientists have seen polar bears pull belugas completely out of the water.

Belugas often travel together in large groups. Beneath the ice, the whales hunt for fish and squid. Sometimes they visit shallow bays and dive to the bottom to feed on clams and octopuses. Belugas have sharp teeth, but they don't chew their food. Instead, they swallow it whole.

Scientists think belugas use echolocation and sound to find their way through the ice. They also use sound to communicate with one another. By blowing air through their blowholes, belugas can whistle, squeal, chirp, and squawk. Sailors who first discovered belugas called them sea canaries because they make so much noise.

Blue Whales

FAMILY: Balaenopteridae
COMMON NAME: Blue whale
GENUS AND SPECIES: *Balaenoptera musculus*
SIZE: Up to 100 feet (30 m) long; 300,000 pounds (136,000 kg)

Blue whales are the largest animals on Earth today, and may be the largest animal that ever lived. Whalers considered these huge creatures a great prize. Before modern whaling, hundreds of thousands of these giant animals roamed the oceans. Today only a few thousand remain.

Blue whales have baleen instead of teeth. When a blue whale feeds, it gulps a great mouthful of water and *krill*—tiny, shrimplike animals. Then it uses its tongue and cheeks to push the water through the long plates of baleen, trapping the krill inside. The whale licks up the krill, swallows, and gulps again. A blue whale eats 8,000 pounds (3,600 kg) of krill a day!

Blue whale calves are the biggest babies in the world. At birth, they measure 25 feet (8 m) and weigh 6,000 pounds (2,700 kg)! Blue whale babies drink about 80 gallons (302 L) of mother's

30

milk each day. In their first few months, the calves gain as much as 200 pounds (90 kg) a day. When calves are about 8 months old, they start catching food on their own.

Blue whales communicate with songs that carry across thousands of miles of water. A whale on one side of the Pacific Ocean might hear a whale "singing" on the other side!

Humpback Whales

FAMILY: Balaenopteridae
COMMON NAME: Humpback whale
GENUS AND SPECIES: *Megaptera novaeangliae*
SIZE: Up to 60 feet (18.5 m) long; 100,000 pounds (45,000 kg)

A humpback whale hurls itself out of the water, twists in midair, and then lands on its back with a thunderous splash. This spectacular leaping is called breaching. Scientists don't know why humpbacks breach. They may be communicating, or they may be scratching an itch. Or maybe humpbacks just love to play!

Humpback whales live in nearly all the world's oceans. In the summer, humpbacks feed in northern waters that are rich with food. In the winter, they move south. Pacific humpbacks spend the winter in Hawaii. Atlantic humpbacks winter in the Caribbean.

The humpback has a special way of catching its food. It makes nets out of bubbles! First, a humpback whale swims under a school of fish. Then it releases a stream of bubbles from its blowhole as it circles the school. The rising bubbles herd the fish together. Then the whale lunges up through the center of the school, gulping a huge mouthful of water and fish.

Many people have heard the humpback's oddly beautiful songs. These whales sing only during the winter months, when they live in warm waters. Humpbacks mate at that time, so they may sing to

32

attract mates or establish territories. Every year, all the whales sing the same song. And every year, it's a different song.

Right Whales

FAMILY: Balaenidae
COMMON EXAMPLE: Northern right whale
GENUS AND SPECIES: *Balaena glacialis*
SIZE: Up to 60 feet (18 m); 21,000 pounds (9,500 kg)

Right whales got their name from whalers who thought they were the "right" whales to catch. Right whales swim slowly, live close to shore, and float when they die. They also have plenty of meat, blubber, and baleen. Whale blubber was a valuable product. It was made into oil for lamps and candles. Baleen, which is stiff but flexible, was made into buggy whips and stiffeners for women's clothes.

Whalers killed so many right whales that the animals are now close to extinction. Researchers estimate that only 300 northern right whales remain in the North Atlantic, and only 3,000 southern right whales inhabit the Southern Hemisphere.

Scientists can recognize an individual right whale by the pattern of white spots on its head and back. The spots are actually patches of scaly skin. They develop just after birth and stay the same throughout the whale's lifetime.

The right whale has a feeding style called skimming. It swims along the surface of the ocean with its mouth open and scoops up water and plankton. The water flows out through the baleen at the back of the mouth, and the plankton sticks to the inside. Most of

the plankton animals that the right whale eats are smaller than a grain of rice. A right whale eats millions and millions of these tiny animals each day.

Gray Whales
FAMILY: Eschrichtiidae
COMMON NAME: Gray whale
GENUS AND SPECIES: *Eschrichtius robustus*
SIZE: Up to 50 feet (15 m); 66,000 pounds (30,000 kg)

People who live along the California coastline often see gray whales. These large cetaceans migrate from the warm waters off Mexico to the cold waters off Alaska and back again. No other mammals travel so far. The whales travel 10,000 to 14,000 miles (16,000 to 22,530 km) round trip!

When they reach the warm lagoons off the Baja Peninsula in Mexico, female gray whales give birth to their calves. The newborns are 16 feet (5 m) long. The baby whales drink their mothers' rich milk and build up blubber for the long journey to the summer feeding grounds in the Arctic Ocean.

Like other baleen whales, gray whales feed on fish and squid. They also feed on the ocean floor. This is called grubbing. Using one side of its jaw, a gray whale stirs up small animals that live in the mud. The whale swims open-mouthed through the cloud of mud and animals, takes a great gulp, and pushes the water out through its baleen. What's left behind is dinner. Gray whales are the only baleen whales that grub for food.

People have hunted gray whales almost to extinction. Today there are no gray whales in the Atlantic Ocean. However, in the 1940s,

36

gray whales were protected, and the hunting of these wonderful
cetaceans stopped. Thousands of gray whales once again swim in
Pacific waters.

Fin Whale

FAMILY: Balaenopteridae
COMMON NAME: Fin whale
GENUS AND SPECIES: *Balaenoptera physalus*
SIZE: Up to 80 feet (24 m) long; 12,000 pounds (5,500 kg)

Thar she blows! When a fin whale returns to the surface after a deep dive, it lets out a great breath of air called a spout. Many people think the spout is water. It's not. Warm, moist air from the whale's lungs forms the spout. A whale's spout can rise more than 50 feet (15 m). On a clear day, whale watchers can spot a spout from more than a mile away.

Fin whales are the second-largest whales. They live in all the world's oceans. Their powerful flukes make them one of the fastest whales on Earth. Fin whales can reach a speed of 23 miles (37 km) per hour.

Like other large whales, fin whales eat a lot. Their favorite foods are krill

and fish. When a fin whale feeds, it takes a few breaths, dives for several minutes, and then surfaces with its mouth wide open. Birds circle overhead and swoop to catch the tiny flapping fish that get away. As the fin whale gulps a giant mouthful of fish and water, grooves on the whale's throat expand. Then the grooves contract and push water through the whale's baleen, trapping the fish inside the whale's mouth. The baleen of fin whales can be up to 3 feet (1 m) long.

A Look at the Future

Would you like to study cetaceans? Researchers have many questions about cetaceans. How many whales are there? Why do some whales beach themselves? What do whales' songs mean? Those are just a few of the questions that scientists want to answer.

Scientists who study cetaceans sometimes journey to exotic locations. Most cetacean research takes place on boats, sometimes far from shore. But scientists cannot always find the cetaceans they want to study. Even when researchers find the whales, tracking them is a challenge. When a cetacean dives, no one knows where it may surface.

Scientists watch a group of orcas.

Researchers often use special tools. Radio tags help scientists study whale movement. Radio tags send out signals that tell scientists how deep whales dive, how fast they swim, and how far they travel.

Scientists have also developed special ways of identifying individual cetaceans. Researchers who study humpbacks look at their tails. Each humpback whale's tail has a special shape and color pattern. Humpback tails are as unique as human fingerprints. Once scientists identify and name a humpback, they can watch that whale for years.

Salt, Pepper, and Notch are just a few of the hundreds of humpbacks that researchers now recognize and follow in the northern Atlantic Ocean. By studying the same whales from year to year, scientists learn more about whale families, where whales travel, and how they grow.

A scientist photographs the tail of a humpback whale.

A scientist listens to recordings of whale sounds.

Scientists also want to learn more about how whales and dolphins communicate. The researchers use underwater microphones to record whale sounds and songs. Sometimes they play human music for the cetaceans to see if the animals will listen.

Most whales, dolphins, and porpoises are protected all over the world today. During the years that they were hunted, many of the animals faced extinction. Today, pollution and fishing cause the biggest problems for cetaceans. People must protect the oceans and rivers where cetaceans live. Maybe one day you will join the effort to learn more about these amazing animals and to protect them and the oceans where they live.

Words to Know

baleen—rows of fringed plates that grow from the upper jaws of baleen whales and strain small animals from the water

blowhole—the opening to the lungs of a cetacean. It is are similar to a the nostrils in humans.

blubber—a layer of fat just below the skin of most marine mammals

carnivore—an animal that hunts and eats other animals

cetacean—a member of an order of mammals that live in water but breathe air

class—a group of creatures within a phylum that share certain characteristics

echolocation—finding distant or invisible objects by bouncing sound waves off the objects

family—a group of creatures within an order that share certain characteristics

flipper—a broad, flat limb adapted for swimming

fluke—a fin on the tail of a whale

genus (plural **genera**)—a group of creatures within a family that share certain characteristics

kingdom—one of the five divisions in which all living things belong: the animal kingdom, the plant kingdom, the fungus kingdom, the moneran kingdom, and the protist kingdom

krill—the small, shrimplike animals eaten by many baleen whales

43

mammal—a type of warm-blooded animal that feeds its young mother's milk

order—a group of organisms within a class that share certain characteristics

plankton—a group of tiny floating plants and animals

phylum (plural **phyla**)—a group of creatures in a kingdom that share certain characteristics

pod—a group of cetaceans

species—a group of creatures within a genus that share certain characteristics.

Learning More

Books

Amos, Stephen H. *Familiar Marine Mammals, North America.* The Audubon Society Pocket Guides. New York: Random House, 1990

Bunting, Eve. *The Sea World Book of Whales.* New York: Harcourt Brace,1980.

Horton, Casey. *Dolphins.* New York: Marshall Cavendish, 1996.

Hoyt, Eric. *Meeting the Whales: The Equinox Guide to Giants of the Deep.* Ontario: Camden House, 1991.

McMillan, Bruce. *Going on a Whale Watch.* New York: Scholastic, 1992.

Papastavrou, Vasilli. *Whale .* New York: Alfred A. Knopf, 1993.

Web Sites

National Marine Fisheries Service
http://kingfish.ssp.nmfs.gov/tmcintyr/cetacean/cetacean.html
This site provides information about laws and programs that protect cetaceans.

Prince of Whales
http://www.princeofwhales.com/virtual/
This site takes you on a virtual whale watch that uses slides to take you on a whale watch adventure.

WhaleNet

http://whale.wheelock.edu/

This site provides information about whales and news about whale events and issues. The site has slide shows, research reports, and great links to other cetacean sites. You can even write in and ask questions of scientists.

Whale Watcher Expert System

http://vvv.com/ai/demos/whale.html

This site uses questions and photos to help identify whales and provides many facts and links.

Index

About the Author

Elizabeth Tayntor Gowell enjoys exploring the ocean and writing about marine life. She is an award-winning author and environmental consultant. Ms. Gowell has worked for the New England Aquarium; the Massachusetts Coastal Zone Management Program; and SEACAMP, a marine science education program in the Florida Keys. Her adventures with cetaceans include leading whale watches, snorkeling with dolphins, and sailing with scientists to study the endangered northern Atlantic right whale. Ms. Gowell lives Rhode Island with her husband, Jay, and her three children—Emily, Matthew, and Julia.